He Carried Me
In The
Dark Places

Doriene Reynolds

He Carried Me
In The
Dark Places

Doriene Reynolds

PUBLISHED BY:
BRENTWOOD CHRISTIAN PRESS
4000 BEALLWOOD AVENUE
COLUMBUS, GEORGIA 31904

Dedication

I dedicate this book to God my Father, Jesus my Savior, and the Holy Spirit my comforter and inspiration.

Secondly, I dedicate this book to my son that was murdered, Jeffrey Alan Coonan, may the memory of him live on forever.

I also would like to dedicate this book to my two remaining sons, Michael Coonan and Robert Allen.

Acknowledgements

I would like to thank the Holy Spirit for speaking to me that which I have written down in this book. I thank God for the hard times and the good times for I have profited by them all.

I would like to thank my family and friends for encouraging me to put these poems and writings into a book.

I would like to thank my Pastor, Steve Dohse, for his love, prayers, and inspiration from some of his sermons and his wife, Julia Dohse, for the inspiration from some of her awesome songs.

Introduction

It was the death of my son that brought me to writing poems. I had never written poems before and had not made a conscience effort to do so. The poems came to me supernaturally without ever having to plan them.

The purpose in publishing my innermost feelings, laying bare my soul, is in hopes that even one poem will touch your heart and change your life, to give you hope to carry on. This is my legacy to whomever reads this book.

People say that Christianity is for the weak, those who need a crouch. The exact opposite is true. It is for the stout hearted, Christianity isn't a live happily forever after pill. It's the presence of joy no matter what the circumstance, the peace that passes understanding, if we will follow His Word (Philippians 4: 4-9). The Comforter, the Holy Spirit, your friend, will always be with you to help you through all things. You are never alone. Think it not strange that bad things happen to us, He *will* turn all things around for good (Romans 8:28) it is not God's intent to bring us harm (Jeremiah 29:11).

These poems and other writings do not necessarily appear in the order that they were written.

Table of Contents

In the Desert Place

Winter Days

Growing in Him

The Divorce

We went to counseling in our
struggle in the marriage.
The problems we had, possibly
from before the carriage.

He had turned to beer for his
pain and perhaps another
woman.
I turned to food for comfort
and religion.

He has his life; I have mine, no
longer a family,
each of us floundering in our
own misery.

Can we go back and begin
again.
I don't know. It would take
HIM.

How do you find love and
happiness when all has failed?
What I have found in my quest
is JESUS.

The Blood

I stood there and saw his blood in the
gutter, that's all there was of him I
could see - that part of me.

I stood there and looked, I yearned to
touch him - that part of me.

Oh, God, now I know how you felt
when your son shed his blood- for
them and me.

Oh, God, may my son's spilled blood
draw others to the spilled blood of
the Lamb who died - for them and
me

A Mother of a Pearl

A grain of sand in a clam is very
painful, but makes a pearl - you see.

My son was chosen to be a pearl of
great price, in his death may God -
you see.

I am a mother of a pearl and I take
this time to say, it is God's peace
that comforts me - you see.

I Got a Glimpse of Heaven

I got a glimpse of Heaven today.
This angel was standing there, arms
bent at the elbow, palms extended
flat.

He was singing Hallelujah praises,
an offering to the King.

What radiance, what peace, joy
unspeakable, words cannot express.

Thank you God, for letting me see
my sons face.

Do Not Weep for Me

Do not weep for me, because I am no
longer with you.

Do not weep for me because what
might have been.

Do not weep for me because I have
gone to Heaven.

Do not weep for me because I am
happier than I ever have been.

I Walk, I Talk, I Eat

I walk, I talk, I eat, and I laugh and
write, life as usual - no not quite.

Thoughts creep in, the stomach
churns, and my dead son's life I
continue to yearn.

He's in Heaven I say, no more grief
to bare and someday soon, I'll be
with him up there.

God's Mercy and Grace

As I sit in this large overstuffed
chair, it encompasses me.

I can get up and leave that restful
place, by choice and sometimes by
necessity but His mercy and grace
goes with me wherever I go.

I also can move away from His
restful place, His mercy and grace.

I choose to keep my mind stayed on
Thee.

That's Not My Baby Boy

Oh dear God, that's a man in there,
not my baby boy.

A body without a soul or spirit is just
a shell of what used to be.

He looks nothing like my baby boy;
that makes it easier to accept.

My baby boy is in Heaven with
Jesus, happier than he has ever been,
just praising Him.

I Buried My Son Today

The world continues to turn, people
going to and fro.

I buried my son today.

I look into their faces, they see me,
but don't even know.

I buried my son today.

There it is that gray steel box,
flowers in perfect array.

I buried my son today.

They come in love with a flower one
by one.

I buried my son today.

I didn't bring a flower; I haven't
been to this kind of thing before.

I buried my son today.

Oh God, what do I do; what do I say.
He said, "Just pray."

I buried my son today.

I touched the steel box where my sons body lay and begun to pray.

I buried my son today.

My prayers were lain upon the golden alter before His throne.

I buried my son today.

My son is in Heaven and can smell the incense *of* my prayer.

I buried my son today.

The flowers that lay over him he cannot smell but my prayers he did smell.

I buried my son today.

I opened my eyes and saw a tear from each eye drop into that hole.

I buried my son today.

I'm glad I didn't have a flower now.

I buried my son today.

A Find

I found my love,
No more to be lonely.

His voice is sweet,
making sour *out of* honey.

His heart more beautiful;
comparing to the red rose.

I long to embrace him;
never *to* let go.

I Found Love

I have a song on my lips,
joy in my heart, and
a dance to my step,
Because I found the one I love.

Thirty years ago I gave my son
up for adoption, not because I
didn't want him but felt best a
couple to give him love.

You can't run away nor forget
that part of you left behind, so
search for him or her, I believe
you'll find true love.

Love with No End

I gave him up at birth
believing the best was done.

I tried to bury my feelings of
longing for my son.

Thirty years passed by; no
longer able to hide or run.

I contacted ALMA and in three
months, the search was done.

He loves me and I love him,
together forever with my son.

I promise with all my heart to
never stop loving or run.

It is Love

Can't remember how long it's
been since I felt quite like this.

I'm filled with love and joy, I
want to sing and dance, what
bliss.

To love and to be loved, best
expressed with a hug and kiss.

Resurrection Day Prayer

On this Resurrection Day for our
sins Christ did pay.

Change me from within; cleanse
me from all sin.

Stay close to me; from my
bondages set me free.

I urge you to make that choice
and together we will rejoice.

Easter Treasure

The world thinks of the Easter
bunny, baskets of chocolate and
eggs to find.

Others think of Jesus' death and
resurrection; treasures of a
different kind.

On Valentines Day

On this Valentines Day, I write
to tell of unconditional love.

Because of pain and sorrow I
continued to face, I couldn't
believe God's continued love.

Why must I strive on in
disgrace?

After much prayer and
reflection,
He said He was bringing me
into perfection.

He pointed me to you, Son and
how deeply I continue to love
you no matter what is said or
done.

He said to me, "this is how I
love but so very much more."

To My Son, Mike

I love you not for what you do
or say, as that can change from
day to day.

I love you because you are apart
of me, more than just a family
tree.

At times I don't like the things
you do; but we all walk to the
beat of a different drum.

My love for you is a forever
thing, just to hear your voice
makes my heart sing.

Missing You In July

This is my first 4th of July spent
without you. Did you think of
me or even have a passing
thought.

To pine for what could be will
leave only depression.

I choose to think on happy
things, as I ought.

Pledge Of Allegiance

Today is a day of celebration.

This is a time to renew our
pledge of allegiance to America.
and to be thankful for our
freedom.

For me, it is also a time to renew
my pledge of allegiance to a
higher kingdom.

I found even greater freedom
than this earth can insure.

It is the kingdom of God. Go
there, I implore.

A Christmas Invitation

I saw Mom crying and
kissing some man's feet
last night.

They didn't see me come
down stairs to have a peek.

They thought I was in my
bed fast asleep.

I didn't know the man and
what I saw gave me a fright.

I asked Mom who he was;
she said, He is Jesus her
Savior.

What great love He has for
Mom and me and you too.

Ask Him to forgive you of
your sins; you too can know
His favor.

Struggling

The days and nights creep so
slowly on.

Struggling to keep in my heart a
song.

Anger, fear, despair, I fight all
day long.

His Word is true; to Him I
belong.

Hold on, keep the faith, and be
strong.

Stay Each Day

I sat upon a stoop one day; like
the birds, wanting to fly away.

God Almighty said, stay.

Lord supply my need for each
day, a home, food, and love
along the way.

God Almighty said, stay.

I continue to exist day after day;
wondering when His blessings
will come my way.

God Almighty said, stay.

Question - Answer

Oh for money for the bills and
want to keep my home still.

Wait He says in His patient
voice; rely on me for your
choice.

How much longer is my plea;
my faith is beginning to flea.

There are lessons you need to
learn; to My Word you must
turn.

I read, I stood, I claimed too;
still no sign of the buckaroo.

It's not only with eyes you see,
thank me and it shall be.

My Cry - Enough

Sorrow misery and pain has
been my middle name.

Fifty years of this stuff, I 'm not
taking anymore guff.

The Christian life is supposed to
bring joy, God send someone
my way is my ploy.

I can't go on taking much more;
can't stop thinking about
forevermore.

Hear my plea.
Don't make me flee.

His Answer

Stay, stay, I'm coming your
way. I'll grant you your seed
enough to last.

Stay, stay, I'm coming your
way.

My Answer

Time is of the essence. Don't
take long.

Tears roll from my
eyes, down my cheeks, and onto
the pillow.

The river stops. The
cry is much deeper than the
surface bellow. .

Nobody sees
the deep misery, not because it
is so well hidden.

They see as
deep as they want to be bidden.

They have no time for others.
Their life is full of their own
pain.

His Reply

Wait, wait, I'll bring my cup.

You will be filled and forget the
past.

Wait, wait, I'll bring my
cup.

He Is Calling For Me

He is calling for me but I
do not answer Him for shame.

He is calling for me but I
am too busy, I exclaim.

He is calling for me as He
desires to reveal His Glory.

Here We Go Again

I've been around this mountain
before; here we go again.

No money, food, or job
available; I've done all I can.

I'm in line for a miracle; it's
under His watchful scan.

What will tomorrow have to
offer; who knows His plan.

A Lovely Swan

I really like swans; why is that;
what is it deep within.

Remember the story of the ugly
duckling that was rejected and
never fit in.

One day it saw some swans and
realized where it belonged.

I'm beginning to discover that
I'm not an ugly duckling but a
lovely swan.

It is a matter of finding your
purpose in this old world.
To discover the talent given you,
and accomplish the purpose for
which you were created.

I Catch On

I'm beginning to catch on; life
does go on.

Maybe not the way we plan; for
it's under His watchful scan.

We sit quietly, thinking we're
praying, when all along it's
really fretting.

If you want some action, don't
concentrate on subtraction.

God's Word is still the same,
search it, it's yours to claim.

The answer isn't always right
away; for often it takes time, so
don't sway.

The Job Experience

Battered from every side, leaves
me wanting to die; suicide is not
the answer, for surely I would
fry.

Friends and relatives look at me
with disgust; for an easier life I
do lust.

They see my troubles as proof of
sin; God is refining, to draw me
to Him.

Life will get better after awhile,
so keep on keeping on and
smile.

Unreturned Love

The pain of sorrow is so great
when others don't love you as
they ought.

We must not let this steal our
joy, the good fight must be
fought.

One day we will leave this earth
and their regrets will not stop.

A Mother's Love

I gave life to him and fed him
from my breast.

His first nine years he showed
me love, unlike the rest.

The teen years he pulled away
from me and my God.

My unconditional love for him
will never end.

There's no love like a mother
has for he children.

A Castaway

Here I am in a field all- alone,
Desolate, a castaway, with no
home.

I'm not what I used to be,
Some parts missing that
changed me.

In years past, when I was a
beauty; I gave of myself, I did
my duty.

Are there eyes to see what I
can be again? Come, hold me,
be a friend.

Doesn't anybody care about
this old rusty car?

Is It Heaven

Creeping down this bumpy road,
clouds of dust are the only
things following me.

No train whistles or whirling
trucks going by in the night
disturbing me.

Only the wind, birds, and
coyotes can be heard calling me.

It Builds Character

Backed into a canyon at the end
of a dusty road.

It builds character, I heard a
friend say.

It is so quiet all I can hear are
my ears ringing.

It builds character, I heard a
friend say.

I sit and wait for God to move or
direct a route.

It builds character, I heard a
friend say.

No job, little food, only a travel
trailer to live in.

It builds character, I heard a
friend say.

Hey, God, how much bigger
does my character have to get.

At The End of An
Old Dusty Road

He fills my senses with a
cooling breeze and the smell of
earth being blown from one
place to the other.

Viewing the crevices of the red
rocky mountain, all kinds of
adventures await there.

Turning of the head, I see cacti,
prickly pears, and mesquite
trees.

There is only the sounds of flies
and bees and the parade of ants
to watch go by.

At night there are the frightening
howls of the coyotes as they
roam for prey.

Down a Dusty Road

He has brought me out here
miles down a dusty road, full of
ruts and deep washes.

Ragged mountains, and the wind
blowing sand and mesquite trees
surround me.

What beauty in this desolate
place, peace and quiet beyond
compare, but Lord, why am I
here?

Are there lessons to be learned
as I await your call, or is it just
for cheer?

The Wonder Of It All

I watch the sun rise and set.
Clouds roll in, drop some rain and leave,
changing the perspective of things.

I listen to the songs of different birds,
the buzz of bees' yellow jackets,
mosquitoes and things.

I smell the dust in the air as the
wind moves the earth from place to place,
tearing down and building things.

The Spider

The spider calls to the fly
come and sit on my bed with me.

There's a beautiful view from here
come and see what I can see.

No says the fly I know your trick
You want dinner, so I will flee.

A Bird's Chatter

What is that little bird saying
That he urgently is conveying,
Not a song but message portraying.
Could it be a warning of danger lurking.

A Lizard

I saw a lizard sunning on a tree.
Along came a moth flitting merrily.
Oops, the lizard at the moth greedily.

My Dogs

There's Samson, lying in the sun
twitching here and there as he dreams.
Not far off Delilah quietly preens.

Samson so massive and strong, a picture of health.
Delilah, delicate it appears, but really stealth.

Delilah has become Samson's friend.
One will hear a sound or smell a critter and
they run off together to defend.

A Baby Pine Tree

While sitting here in my
reclining chair; I gaze at the
beauty of this snowy dawn.
There is a tall thin baby pine
swaying in the wind, the older
more stately ones only looking
on.

Standing near by is a very tall
motherly pine very laden with
snow, gently swaying, seeming
saying, don't worry little one the
burden will soon be gone.

Ice Cycles

Gazing out my window, ice
cycles I see.

They look like someone
wrapped a thin wire around
them.

Why is it I thought they were
always smooth and this sight
looks so strange to me.

Some of them are dripping, yet
others are not. Are they getting
longer as they drip or shorter be.

Perhaps if I watch long enough I
will be able to see.

As time passes on, I remember
ice cycles as a child and how I
would suck on them as if filled
with sugar flavors. I wonder
why that satisfied me.

As I continue to ponder the ice
cycle drip, I have *come to* the
conclusion whether I see the
drip or not, they all ever so
slowly elongated be.

The Purpose Of Snow

The sky is white as if a
reflection from the earth this
winter day.

The whiteness is washing all the
strife and stress away.

The snow will melt and then we
will be off again bustling about.

The stress and tension begin to
mount.

God in His grace will bring
another white day to give us
time to stop and think.

What Is Heaven Like

I query what is Heaven like.

Are there beautiful snow white
days, colorful autumn leaves,
warm summer rains, and a
gentle breeze through the pines.
Probably not.

I know, that a brilliant light will
illuminate from the Father and
Son.

Will I miss the beauty of this
earth once I am gone.
Probably not.

Why I Am Thankful

My Daddy was killed in the
war when I was only two.

Was a victim of incest at five,
other times too.

Date raped at eighteen;
married and had a baby.

Another attempted rape on this
fair lady.

Lived a loose life; became
pregnant and had an abortion.

Got married for love but he
wanted more than his portion.

Met an intelligent guy; we
married and had a family.

He said I was too religious and
too fat and after fourteen years
he divorced me.

Our two sons didn't want
religion; so with their Father
was quartered.

Two years later our older son
was murdered.

A year later Mom had her
second stroke and died.

After 10 jobs in two years and
unable to find work, Mom's
home I occupied.

Thirty years after his birth, I
found my first- born son.

We found peace in establishing
a reunion.

Tormented with fear and
depression the pounds
multiplied.

But Now

I am forgiven of my wicked
past.

Jesus said, repent, and I will
give you peace at last.

He gives me reason to sing and
dance.

I have a new life, a second
chance.

You don't have to be good to
receive His mercy and grace.

Just humble yourself and He
will lift you to His Heavenly
Place.

There are still hard times
because we were thrown out of
the garden.

Jesus was crucified, died, and
went to Heaven.

Then sent the Holy Spirit to
comfort us.

An Alien

I am from a different world,
that is why I don't fit in.

I come from a place of beauty,
there is *no* strife within.

In my veins instead of blood,
is a river that flows.

In my inner most being,
the Spirit of God grows.

Warfare

I'm a doer of the word
not just a hearer only.

I put my feet to work and
cut out the baloney.

I walk streets of the city
Satan is whom I fight.

In warfare, I show no pity
demonic forces must take flight.

It's not by my power or might
but by the Holy Spirit.

Prayer Of Praise

Lord you are my God and
I praise your Holy Name.

You have changed me, I
will never be the same.

You are my refuge when I am
poor and in distress.

In your mercy, you
always bless.

The Baby is Dead

The baby is dead. How can this
be?

How could this happen, what
made life flee?

Take me back to this baby; I will
not let it die!

Awake! I say. Awake!
My baby, my dreams and
visions; I lost in the strife.

Resurrection has come; now I
can see.

No Words

Words have been spoken in so
many ways in love, praise, and
worship.

There is nothing new I could
say, see this heart of clay.

Thanks for the part of you,
Daddy, that created this little
lady.

Thanks for that part of you,
Brother, that is closer than any
other.

Thanks for that part of you.
Mother, with hugs and kisses
forever.

Proper Alinement

My emotions controlled me
no hope could I see.

He is now in control and I am
set free.

On His Word I depend;
everything else fades away.

Lay it all on the alter; no need to
fret, He won't lead you astray.

Nothing Else Matters

I was being stripped once
again. The last of my
possessions were being
asked. I was angry with God.
My Pastor said, "Nothing
else matters."

I couldn't let go of my
possessions without anger. A
year later, sincerely seeking
His face, I began to see that
nothing else matters.

Being in the River Glory is
all I need. His presence,
power, peace, and love, is all
I want, nothing else matters.

I invite you to seek His face;
that's when everything falls
into place and the blessings
come and nothing else
matters.

Draw Me To You

Dear Lord fill me with your
presence; daily abide.

Burn away all that is not of
you, your face, do not hide.

I want to know you; give me
direction.

Your voice I want to hear,
leading me into perfection

I come to you Lord, upon
your firey hill.

Humbly I plea, for your
presence fill.

He Is My Song

My heartaches from lack of
love, I want to cry, I want to
cry.

Jesus, lift me up on your
wings, I want to fly, I want to
fly.

You heard my plea and took
me, above the clouds, above
the clouds.

I sing, not for what I see but
what will be, what will be.

The Dancers

We are the sons and daughters of praise,
with tambourines and streamers ablaze.

We go before where warriors trod,
no need for sword or rod.

We know the victory has been won,
praise and worship is our gun.

We bow and twirl in agile dance,
defeating the enemy in advance.

In My Bridegroom's Presents

My heart is awakened with a
flaming torch,
for the coming of my Bridegroom
on the porch.

He listens to the cry of my
heart in the night,
flowing in oneness until daylight.

His presence brings a stillness
to my heart,
together forever never to part.

A Bronco Ride

I saw my life like a bucking bronco ride,
Being flung up in the air,
then down in despair.

I held on tight through the storm.
My strong right hand gripping
the saddle horn.

The weaker left hand held high
to God for balance.

There would be a quick turn
to the left and then to the right.
I was heard screaming and
crying in fright.

This wasn't fun!
I was beginning to weaken.

I grabbed a hold of God
with both hands.

He lifted me up on His wings.
Now I do soar
above the clouds forevermore.

Contented

My chest is full and puffed up,
filled with much happiness.

I always have food to eat and a
place to rest.

I have clothing to protect me in
the day and night.

I sing because I'm happy and I
sing for your delight.

I was created by, God the Father
and His Son.

I am your red-breasted feathery
friend, a robin.

Duck or Truck

I always felt like and ugly duck;
with legs and neck skinny and
long.

My voice sounded more like a
truck; I just wanted to belong.

I found others like me, what
luck; now I feel like a song.

Striving For The Gold

The struggles have been many.
I compete not for money.

I've been training for an
Olympic game *of* a different
kind.
I know the gold I will find.

It has been many years in the
coming.
For the prize, I continue
running.

There was the death of a son and
mother soon to follow.
Failures with jobs, finances, and
relationships, in self- pity I did
wallow.

At times, for death I did cry.
Jesus answered, get up on my
wings and fly.

On His wings the view is
different.
I now hold life more reverent.

His strength and peace cause me
to abound.
Someday soon, I'll receive the
golden crown.

I Am Justified

My hope lives not because I am not a sinner,
but because I am a sinner for whom
Christ died.

My trust in Christ is not because I am holy;
but being unholy, His righteousness supplied.

My faith rests not upon what I am,
shall be, feel, or know; but who Christ is,
has done, and is doing through me.

Upon Christ's wings of justice and hope,
this fair maiden is set free.

I Lay Me Down To Sleep

I lay me down at night to sleep,
trusting in God my soul to keep.

I ask God's angels to stand
by my bed,
keeping guard over me
in the nights dread.

In the middle of the night when
sleeplessness persists,
my Beloved communes with me
in the nights bliss.

In His grace He removes all stress,
once again to bask in His rest.

Traveling On His Highway

I strive to trust in Jesus
pushing aside all doubt.
In prosperity or adversity,
sickness or health,
popularity or contempt.
His purpose shall be worked out.

Wherever He leads,
I know He has gone before me.
At times, I don't know which way to go,
but I know who goes with me.

The roads I must travel are not always easy,
but it is better to keep moving forward in Him
than sit and become lazy.

Where He takes me, I need not fear
for I know His purpose is pure.
He desires to take me from Glory to Glory,
so I may become more mature.

A Flaming Torch and Trumpet

I am going to let my flaming torch shine.
When others look at me, they will know
I have been with Jesus.

I am as an instrument boldly trumpeting His
wondrous works.
I will blow my trumpet, declaring Christ
Divine.

Back and Forth

I sit on my porch swing every
day and go back and forth,
back and forth.

I sit and watch the people
every day, go back and forth,
back and forth.

The things I see would
stagger your imagination as
they go back and forth, back
and forth.

It didn't take long to see that
nobody noticed me, as they
go back and forth, back and
forth, not really going
anywhere.

I Heard Their Blood Crying (9-11-01)

I heard their blood crying, crying, crying.
What is this that has happened to me?

I cannot be dead; I haven't lived my life to
the end. How can this be?

Where are my family and friends?
I know they will help me.

The cry in my heart, is to say once more,
I love you.

How could anyone hate so much, to have no
regard for the living.

God forgive them, for they know not what
they do.

I heard their blood crying, crying, crying.

A Call to the Nehemiah's in the Land

In the Bible Nehemiah had heard his beloved city was in great danger. The wall surrounding the city of Jerusalem had fallen down. This left them with no form of protection from their enemies. The King gave Nehemiah permission to go and rebuild the wall.

In January of 1991 there had been another violent death of a teenager killing another teenager in the city where I lived. My fifteen year old son had been shot to death one year earlier so I was more aware than some that this made the eighth teen murder. When I heard this on the news, I began to cry and pray to the God of Heaven for my people who have committed these horrible sins of murder, "Oh, God, hear my prayer and stop the slaughter of our youth."

A short time later I met a man who had walked many cities in the world doing spiritual warfare. I had asked him to pray for me for discernment. As he prayed, I realized I was being commissioned by God to walk my city.

I bought some walking boots, a map, and began my plan. Like Nehemiah, who began to rebuild the wall in a counter clockwise direction and at the dung gate, I began walking the perimeter of my city in a counter clockwise direction and at the milk farms.

As I was walking, I would stop and talk to the people about why I was walking; and sometimes I prayed with them. One lady rededicated her life to Christ. I met a twenty one year old young man who had just gone back to high school to complete his education He had been on drugs and wrecked his life. Then he accepted Jesus at the Power Team Evangelistic Outreach. He was having problems with his Christian walk because he was still associating with the same friends. I prayed with him and spent sometime to disciple him. We parted to go our separate ways, hugged, excited how God had brought us together.

I met two young boys. Their mothers were Christians but they weren't going to church and their brothers and sisters were on drugs; and they asked me to pray for them. They continued to ride their bikes with me for about a mile. I told them how God would help them with their schoolwork. They went home but one boy came back to show me his Bible.

I also got to talk to a group of teenage boys standing on a corner by their high school smoking cigarettes. I warned them of the importance of making wise choices of the friends they choose.

While Nehemiah and the people of the city rebuilt the wall they carried their sword for protection. My sword was the Word of God.

I limited my daily walk to two miles in a forward direction. While I walked, I would bind Satan and the evil powers and principalities in the heavenlies and in this present darkness. On the way back to my car, I would claim God's word of salvation to the families, Holy boldness to the Christians and revival in the land.

We must be faithful to the call of God. One person can make a difference with prayer, in faith.

Who will rise up to the call? We must get together and build a wall of protection around our cities and neighborhoods. It's a matter of life and death. It could be your teenage son or daughter tomorrow. We must rise up in the name of Jesus; prepare for battle, pull down the strongholds of murder, death, hatred, rebellion, witchcraft, Satanism, etc. Then we must call for revival in the land.

Go forth in the name of Jesus!

The Earthen Vessel

The purchaser of a pot no longer wanted it. He felt the pot was too big and religious so he cast it away. The pot landed on the Rock and broke in two large pieces. Love picked it up and with a slip of clay, repaired it.

Two smaller matching pots got separated. One stayed with the purchaser and the other stayed with the pot. Later the little pot wanted to go the purchaser, so the pot let it go. The pot was thrown upon the Rock, again, breaking it into a few more pieces. Love picked the pot up and mended it.

The pot began to be used but every time it found a job to do, it got thrown on the Rock and broken. Each time the pot was dropped, and more broken, Love would pick it up and repair it.

The little pot that had originally stayed with the purchaser got shot and was unable to be repaired. Love gently picked up the little pot and said, I'll keep it for me. The big pot went crashing down on the Rock and shattered into many pieces. Love quickly came and scooped up the many fragmented pieces and said I can fix it. It took time and patience of which Love had a lot.

The pot was used once again but never quite the same. You could see all the mended places. It lost most of its beauty.

The pot found refuge in a Temple. Some how there was some tugging and pulling and the pot was dropped on the Rock once again. This time it was completely shattered. Love most tenderly, picked the pieces up and just held them. With great indignation, Love said He would not let it be destroyed. With the tears in His eyes, he watered down the clay pieces and began to reform the pot. The pot was made into a different vessel. It was like new. Originally, it was made with water to be formed but this time was made with the tears of Love, no more patches, it was stronger than before. Love put the pot into the fire to strengthen it, and He painted it. It was a thing of beauty once again.

A pot shattered into many pieces can become new but it must yield itself to the Rock, and none other, if it is to be a vessel fit for use. Love is the only one who can make it new.

Matthew 21:14: He who falls on this stone will be broken to pieces, but he on whom it falls will be crushed.

My Time in the Desert

It was time for me to leave the high country and head South to warmer weather, but I didn't have the money or gas for my car or money to pay someone to move my travel trailer. Finally, one day a couple from the church I was attending, said I could stay on their property. They pulled my travel trailer down there for me, and got me setup. This place was a very old farm backed into a canyon with no phone. The nearest neighbor was eight miles away. The long dusty road was full of deep washes gutted out from the runoff when it rained. There gate at the property line was one mile to the farmhouse. That part of the road was even worse; it was almost, impossible to maneuver.

With no money, the only food I got, was whatever was given to me. It reminded me of Elijah by the brook, being feed by the ravens. I found a new friend, who occasionally gave me some money, which was enough for a package of hamburger meat and a bag of food for my dogs, Samson and Delilah. Suddenly the money stopped. It wasn't long before all the food was gone. There was nothing to give to my dogs so I took them to the Humane Society, being St Bernard's, I knew they would get a home right away.

A short time after I got home from taking my dogs to the Humane Society, my youngest son, Michael, came by to visit as my friends, Prudy and Eileen, in a distant town where worried because they couldn't get a hold of me and asked him to come and check on me. Since the fence was always locked he had to climb the fence and walk a mile in where I was parked. Right away he asked where the dogs were and I told him with tears pouring down my face. I was so glad to see him in particular, as I missed him so much but also because I hadn't seen anyone for a while. Michael lived at college in a nearby town and he had to turn right a round and go back.

The next week he came with his girl friend and said, "Let's go." He said that he got the dogs out of the pound for me and he would buy the dog food for them. Wow, did I cry.

Two weeks later they ran a way together. I searched and searched the wilderness for them for days and then finally gave up. My son, Michael, came to the rescue again. Someone had found the dogs and because they had their tags, was able to get a hold of my son. He wasn't too thrilled walking back to my trailer again. We went to the man's house that found them but he wasn't home. We went to the corner Circle K and called. There was no answer, but just as he hung up, the man came around the corner with the dogs in the back of his truck. We yelled and waved our arms and he saw us and brought us to his home. He wanted to keep the dogs, especially Samson, as he was so beautiful. I had owned him for six years but I owned Delilah for six months. I let him keep Delilah, she liked running and I know Samson would never have left if it weren't for her. Does this sound like a familiar Bible story?

My dog and I would go for long walks in the desert. Rattlesnakes greeted us one day and I saw my share of tarantula and scorpions but we were always safe.

My car ran out of oil, there wasn't even a drop on the dipstick, and I had no money to even buy one quart of oil. The daughter of the owners property where I was staying told me I could get gas at the station that her and her husband owned. That was so wonderful. When my new friend stopped sending me money, this same couple gave me money a few times, it was the same amount.

The owner of the property came by to make sure I was all right. I told him with tearful frustration about the oil and he gave me 3 quarts he had in the barn. Shortly after that my water pump went out. I couldn't keep water in the car. I decided I had to do something or ruin the engine, so I went to that gas station and got some *stop* leak, taking them up on their generous offer. A short time later, he came down to check on his horse because one of the horses had a bad leg and he had to doctor it We talked a couple of evenings and one night had a steak dinner, I think he knew I didn't have much to eat.

I was told there was a pass through the mountains that led all the way up to a town 50 miles North from where I was. I couldn't see it; and Samson and I walked all around that desert place. Once I got lost but there happened to be this scruffy man there and he pointed me right to where my trailer was. I had to walk through tall grasses up to my hips not knowing what might be in there. I felt a little uneasy about that man knowing exactly were my trailer was. I felt like I was an Israelite wondering in the desert, and I complained like them too. But the Lord gave me manna and protected me. The coyotes howling at night, was pretty frightening, and at times they came pretty close.

God was always near, speaking His peace to me.

There was no phone line out that way, therefore, it was hard to get a job. I decided to go visit my long time friend, Prudy, and she invited me to stay with her, which I did do.

I went back to get most of my things and the owner was there and asked me to get the trailer off their property. I asked her to take it back up north to my property; and told her I would pay them as soon as I could for moving the trailer for me.

I did a Bible study on trials and discovered that sometimes He allows trials in our life to test our heart. I had learned to trust in God to meet all my needs. The wondering in the desert, came to an end.

I Had a Dream

(Read Luke 22: 35-46 first)

I was at a gas station where my husband worked but he wasn't doing anything; he was just standing there. He wasn't serving the customers. He didn't even put gas in the people's cars!

I was feeling very unhappy and lonely so I decided to go for a walk. I had walked for a long while, about 10 miles. I was at a traffic light and this good looking man on a motorcycle looked at me as if he could see right into my heart and he asked me if I wanted a ride. I immediately said yes.

I hopped on the cycle and wrapped my arms around his waist so I wouldn't fall off when he took-off, I had never been on a motorcycle before. This man had on a beautiful royal blue silk shirt and pants. I felt compelled to lay my head on his back. There was an overpowering flow of love and peace emanating from him. I don't want this ride to end I thought, as we rode toward the destination I had given him.

We arrived at the gas station and I immediately dismounted the motorcycle and began to walk away. The man on the motorcycle called to me, "Come away with me." I said, "I can't, I am married. See, he is my husband, I continued," as I pointed to him. The man on the motorcycle looked at me with great pain in his deep brown eyes and he drove away.

I once again felt this sad, lonely feeling. I decided to walk away again but this time I went in another direction. There was a strip mall and I decided to walk in there. I couldn't be seen, as there was a building between the mall and the road.

Suddenly the same man on the motorcycle pulled up in front of me, got off his motorcycle and came over *to me*. I was shocked to see him. The thought raced through my mind, "how did he know where I was, I didn't think I could be seen from the road."

He gently grabbed my shoulders and pulled me to him. He pulled my head to his chest as he said; "I want you to hear my heartbeat for you." His heart was beating with great passion. It was overwhelming. He once again took my shoulders and moved me away from him so I could look into his face. His heart was so full he could hardly speak but stumbling he spoke; "I. I." Then he gently held my head in his hands, and he kissed me on the lips. The power of his gentle kiss was so awesome my knees buckled and I could barely stand. With his hands still holding my head, he said with a longing in his voice I will never forget, "I want you to be my bride." The End

After hearing this dream, my Pastor said that the man at the gas station was symbolic of the things of this world we hold on to. The man on the motorcycle is Jesus. This dream is about the passion Jesus has for the lost.

I Love God And I Pray Every Day But I Hate Church

This statement made in the title comes from a wounded spirit or someone who has been hurt by the church. The reason I say that is because, the words, I hate church, contradicts what a person who loves God would say.

The definition of church according to the Webster Dictionary: Lords house, a building for public worship, one of Christian worship.

Matthew 12:18: And I tell you that you are Peter, and on this rock I will build my church and the gates of hell will not overcome it.

Ephesians 2:19 and 20: Consequently you are no longer foreigners and aliens, but fellow citizen with God; people and member of Gods household built on the foundation of the apostles and prophets, with Christ Jesus himself as the chief cornerstone.

The meaning of cornerstone in the Webster Dictionary: a stone at the corner of a building beginning the erection of a building, the basic or main part of the building, the foundation.

If you say you hate the church, you are saying you hate the cornerstone, or the church of Jesus Christ.

The Body of Christ

The body of Christ and those who claim to be Christians and those claiming belief in, and allegiance to Christ is also called the church.

I Timothy 4:11 thru 15: Command and teach these things. Don't let anyone look down on you because you are young, but set an example for love, in faith and in purity. Until I come, devote yourself to the public reading of scripture, to preaching, and to teaching Do not neglect your gift given to you

The Webster Dictionary meaning of devotes: to dedicate, to apply oneself to some purpose.

This is a command, not if you feel like it.

Imitators Of Christ

Christ attended the temple to gather together with others.

Mark 1:21 they went to Capernaum, and when the Sabbath came, Jesus went into the synagogue and began to teach.

Acts 13: 14 thru 15: From Perga they went on to Pisidian Antioch. On the Sabbath they entered the synagogue and sat down. After reading from the Law and Prophets, the synagogue rulers sent word to them, saying, brother, if you have a message of encouragement for the people, please speak.

Hebrews 10:25: Let us not give up meeting together, as some are in the habit of doing but let us encourage one another, and all the more as you see The Day approaching

The reason we are to attend church is found in the Bible not man's book of rules.

Deuteronomy 12:5 thru 7: But you are to seek the place the Lord your God will choose from among all your tribes to put His name there for His dwelling. To that place you must go there bringing your burnt offerings and sacrifices, your tithes and special gifts and your freewill offerings. There in the presence of the Lord your God, you and your families shall eat and shall rejoice in everything you have put your hand to, because the Lord your God has blessed it.

Psalm 84:4: Blessed are those who dwell in your house. They are ever praising you.

Luke 4: 16: He went to Nazareth, where he had been brought up, and on the Sabbath day he went into the synagogue, as was His custom.

Christ and the disciples went to the church to teach.

John 6:59: He said this while teaching in the synagogue in Capernaum.

Acts 13:5: When they arrived at Salamis, they proclaimed the Word of God in the Jewish synagogue. John was with them as their helper.

Acts 14:1: At Iconium Paul and Barnabas went as usual into the Jewish synagogue.

Jesus Christ went to the temple as a little boy and taught there. He got angry at those making a profit selling pigeons etc. for sacrifices, yet He continued to go to the Temple. The Priests came against Him and finally had Him killed. Even then, He had compassion on them and asked God the Father to forgive them. Christ loved man enough to die for us, even those who killed Him.

John 13:1: Now before the Feast of the Passover, when Jesus knew that His hour had come that He should depart from this world to the Father, having loved His own who were in the world, He loved them to the end.

Someone in the church might have lied against you or treated you unfairly. There are many things that could happen but not to the point of killing you.

Leviticus 19:18: Do not seek revenge or bear a grudge against one of your people, but love you neighbor as yourself:

Proverbs 10:12: Hatred stirs up dissension, but love covers over all wrongs.

I John 2:9: Anyone who claims to be in the light but hates his brother is still in the darkness.

I John 3:15: Any one who hates his brother is a murderer, and you know that no murderer has eternal life in him.

If we hold hurt feelings against anyone in the church that is still anger.

Webster Dictionary meaning for hurt: to cause pain or injury, harm, damage or have pain.

Webster Dictionary meaning of anger: hostile reeling because of injury pain.

Church the Bride

The church is as a Bride of Christ; Christ is the Bridegroom. Are you saying you hate the Bride? Christ gave His life for His Bride, the church

II Corinthians 11:2: I am jealous for you with a Godly jealousy. I promised you to one husband, to Christ, so that I might

present you as a pure virgin to him. We are members of His body. We are in union with Him.

Romans 7:4: Therefore my brethren, you also have become dead to the law through the body of Christ, that you may be married to another- to Him who was raised from the dead, that we should bear fruit to God.

Church a Family

We are a part of the family of God. As believers we have been chosen, adopted into this family.

Deuteronomy 14:2: for you are a people holy to the Lord your God. Out of all the peoples on the face of the earth, the Lord has chosen you to be his treasured possession.

John 1:12: Yet to all who received Him, to those who believed in His name, He gave the right to become children of God

We are the children of God, joint heirs with Christ. We are united with the Saints in Heaven. Do you hate the Saints in Heaven?

Church People are Hypocrites

For Christ's sake we may have to suffer some trials.

Matthew 5:11: Blessed are you when people insult you, persecute you and falsely say all kinds of evil against you because of me.

We are to surrender our life to Christ daily. If we truly are dead to Christ, then we no longer take offense.

Galatians 2:20: I have been crucified with Christ and I no longer live, but Christ lives in me. The life I live in the body, I live by faith in the Son of God, who loves me and gave himself for me.

It isn't important who is right or wrong but is the issue of a heart attitude? We are to be in unity, in brotherly love. If you have to apologize and ask for forgiveness for you reactions, you are not admitting you are wrong or defeated. We are to be committed to a life of reconciliation as Christ.

Webster Dictionary meaning of reconciliation: to make friendly again, to make acquiescence.

Webster Dictionary meaning of acquiescence: to consent without protest, to gain by ones own efforts.

People usually don't come to God when everything is going well and life is great. No they usually wait until they are in a crisis; they come in their moment of despair or a lifetime of despair. The church is like a hospital for the wounded. Everyone is in a different place of emotional healing Because some are not entirely healed of their wounds, sometimes things are said or done that hurt others. Yet, some have received completed emotional healing and are able to reach out to others and help them find the help they had received. They are not hypocrites, but in the process of becoming more like Jesus Christ.

We aren't to judge one another, who is sincere and who is not.

Matthew 7:3: Why do you look at the speck of sawdust in your brother's eye and pay no attention to the plank in your own eye.

All of man has sin in their life. Jesus is the only one without sin. If you see someone in sin, pray for him.

I John 5:16: If anyone sees his brother commit a sin that does not lead to death, he should pray and God will give him life.

Christ came not for the righteous but for the sinners. No one is righteous within himself. It is only through the blood of Christ, can we consider ourselves righteous.

Matthew 9:13: All of our own goodness is as filthy rags.

Isaiah 64:6: You cannot earn your way into heaven; it is a free gift of grace through repentance and acceptance of the forgiveness given us through the death and resurrection of Christ.

Church is a Social Club

Some say the church is nothing but a social club. Church is a social meeting place but it is not only that. Our number one purpose in life on this earth is to praise and worship God the

Father, Jesus and the Holy Spirit. Our second purpose is to witness to others what Christ has done for us and what our hope in living is about.

We can praise and worship God at home but there is a stronger presence of God when we come together and praise Him as one body. I would ask you who don't go to church, when was the last time you sang songs of praise to God at home and bowed down on your knees and worshiped Him? If you don't go to church maybe God has someone for you to encourage, or pray for and because you didn't go to church, you didn't meet them for that to happen. The same is true in the reverse, you missed out on a blessing through others because you weren't there to receive it. Also, as we are with other Christians, we don't feel we are in this battle against Satan alone. We pray for one another and fight the good fight together.

Look At Jesus Not Man

Ask the Holy Spirit to direct you to the church He wants you to be apart. Sometimes we go to just any church and maybe that is not the one that is right for you. God has a special church family picked out for you. Pray and ask God where He wants you to go.

Ephesians 4:16: From Him the whole body, joined and held together by every supporting ligament, grows and builds itself up in love, as each part does it's work

Hebrews 10:23: Let us hold unswervingly to the hope we profess for He who promised is faithful. And let us consider how we may spur one another on toward love and good deeds. Let us not give up meeting together, as some are in the habit of doing but let us encourage one another and all the more as you see The Day approaching.

Satan Doesn't Want You in Church

Satan will cause you to sleep-in, get sick, have to work, etc. There are times when he has us get our priorities out of order. The reason he does this is because he knows you will grow in knowledge in how to defeat him and you will become stronger in your resistance to his ways.

Satan was the head of praise in Heaven before he got kicked out. He cannot stay in the place of praise to God

While in church, singing praises to God, we forget about our problems, physical pain, and the bad things that are happening in our lives. There we learn how to change our reactions to our problems and other people. We learn in church how to apply the Bible to our everyday lives.

Invitation to Church

The Head of the Church, the Cornerstone, Christ, invites you to join with His Body, His Bride, in praise, worship and for teaching and for learning.